# ATTACHMENT THEORY:  AN INTRODUCTION FOR

# SOCIAL WORKERS

**Gillian Schofield**

**Social Work Monographs, Norwich**

**First published 2002**

**Reprinted 2003, 2004, 2005**
**2006 and 2007**

Monograph 197

ISBN 1 85784 094 1

# CONTENTS

The Author:   Gillian Schofield is Deputy Director of the Centre for Research on the Child and Family, University of East Anglia

# INTRODUCTION

In recent years there has been a resurgence of interest in attachment theory and a renewed recognition of its particular relevance for child care social work practice. The need to turn to such a relationship-based developmental framework has arisen primarily because of the current emphasis on child development and parenting capacity as a focus in all aspects of child care social work assessment, planning and intervention. The Children Act 1989 stresses the importance of evidence of development in determining need (CA 1989 s.17) and significant harm (CA 1989 s.31). The welfare check list (CA 1989 s.1) also gives a key role to the assessment of children's development. At both policy and practice levels there have been a number of government initiatives, such as *Looking After Children* (Parker et al 1991), the *Framework for Assessment of Children in Need and their Families* (Department of Health 2000) and *Quality Protects* (Department of Health 1999), which require children's development to take centre stage. In this context, it is not surprising that the education and training of social workers on both the Diploma in Social Work and the Post Qualifying Child Care Award also highlight the importance of knowledge of developmental theory and research. But finally, and perhaps most significantly, social workers themselves continue to need ways of making sense of the mass of information which they have about vulnerable children and their families in order to understand the past and the present and to predict the likely future. As David Howe has said, there is nothing so useful as a good theory for helping social workers make sense of what they know (Howe 2001).

But given the need for a developmental theory that can assist in making sense of children and families , why specifically should attachment theory prove so useful?

- Attachment theory offers a framework for understanding the consequences of relationships across time and within families. It uses a life-cycle and intergenerational approach (Fonagy et al 1991a), relevant for understanding how children respond to different kinds of caregiving and how parents (birth, step, foster and adoptive) may replicate or attempt to resist replicating their own experiences of caregiving.

- Attachment theory helps to explain the impact of separation and loss of family relationships (Bowlby 1969, 1973, 1980), a significant part of the experience of many troubled children and families who come to the attention of social services departments.

- Attachment theory, as it has developed in the last two decades, provides a powerful framework for understanding the impact of abuse and neglect on children and the persistent impact of such early adversity on their subsequent relationships into adult life (Crittenden and Ainsworth 1989, George 1996)

- Secure attachment has been seen as a primary goal in areas of social work practice, notably the world of family placement. It has been widely used in research and practice since Bowlby gave evidence to the Curtis committee on fostering in 1946 (BAAF 1999, Cairns 2002, Fahlberg 1994, Howe 1996, Howe et al 1999, Schofield 1998b, Schofield 2003, Schofield and Brown 1999, Schofield et al 2000).

- Most recently, the goal of 'secure attachment to safe and effective carers' has been the focus of the first objective of Quality Protects (Department of Health 1999), a Government initiative for all children in need.

- Attachment theory also helps make sense of the links between the quality of family relationships and the quality of relationships with peers, partners and the outside world- including social workers. It is thus much more than a theory of family relationships.

At its simplest, attachment theory is most powerful in offering a framework for understanding the impact of the past on the present. As Bowlby (1951: 114) put it:

> *Children are not slates from which the past can be rubbed by a duster or sponge, but human beings who carry their previous experiences with them and whose behaviour in the present is profoundly affected by what has gone before.*

Throughout the life span we carry the impression of all that has gone before, in all areas of our lives but particularly in our close relationships. Even ecological models that stress the role of the bigger systems of culture, political processes and the social environment (Bronfenbrenner 1979) and feature as part of the assessment triangle (Department of Health

2

2000), have at their centre the micro-systems of intimate relationships (Schofield 1998a). Experience in relationships is therefore at the heart of much social work assessment and planning. Social workers therefore need to be competent in making sense of those experiences and their impact on development. Attachment theory offers a useful framework to assist in this process but needs to be carefully understood and applied.

This introduction to attachment theory will begin by describing the key elements in attachment theory that explain the formation of secure and insecure attachment patterns and the likely effect of such patterns in childhood, adolescence, adulthood and parenthood. It will include the impact of early abuse and neglect in creating behavioural and relationship difficulties. The focus here is on attachment theory as originated by Bowlby (1969, 1973, 1980, 1988) and then developed by Ainsworth et al (1978), Carlson et al (1989), Cicchetti and Rogosch (1997) Crittenden (1992, 1995), Crittenden and Claussen (1999), Fonagy (1996, 1999, 2000), Fonagy et al (1991a,b) George (1996), George and Solomon (1989, 1996) Main (1991, 1994, 1995), Main and Solomon (1986), Sroufe (1997), Steele and Steele (1994), van IJzendoorn (1996). It is an introduction to some of this rich literature and highlights some of the practice issues for social work that arise from it. Those who wish to go on to apply attachment theory in their day-to-day work would be well advised also to read a more detailed account that relates attachment theory to social work practice (Howe et al 1999). Attachment theory has a great deal to offer to social work practitioners, but it is a complex and subtle theory for understanding complex and subtle processes in human social development. It repays careful study.

# THE ORIGINS OF ATTACHMENT THEORY

## Bowlby and the origins of attachment theory

John Bowlby was a psychiatrist and psychoanalyst. His theoretical framework was remarkable in drawing not only on psychoanalysis but also on ethology, biology and evolutionary theory as a way of theorising how human beings become social beings through their relationships (Bowlby 1969, 1973, 1980). Bowlby's contention in attachment theory is that the quality of early experiences in relationships with caregivers, and the experience of separation and loss of those relationships, shape the self and the quality of later relationships in distinctive ways. This has become an important part of our understanding of individual differences in relationships, not only within families, but also in peer relationships and relationships of all kinds.

The starting point of Bowlby's theory is an evolutionary one, in that infants are said to have a biological drive to *seek proximity* to a protective adult, usually the primary caregiver, in order to survive. This innate drive leads to *attachment behaviour*, crying in early infancy, but moving on to following, smiling and other behavioural strategies in order to achieve proximity to the attachment figure. Attachment behaviour is most in evidence when the infant feels 'threatened, endangered or stressed' (George 1996: 412).

The *quality* of the attachment relationship can best be understood by emphasising the highly significant role of *anxiety about the availability of caregivers in the face of stress or danger* which drives the infant's behaviour (Goldberg 2000, Howe et al 1999). For the *securely* attached infant, that anxiety is allayed by the sensitive responsiveness of the caregiver. The process of building a secure attachment relationship relies on the repetition over time of a process in which the child experiences a *sensitive and predictable response* from this caregiver to the child's signals. If caregiver responses are both predictable and accurately meet the needs of the child - in the form of physical and emotional care, protection and availability - then the child can feel safe. Anxiety about hunger, cold and other risks and

dangers will not overwhelm the child and the emotional and cognitive connection with the attachment figure will be maintained. Although anxiety about physical and emotional availability is the key to the early development of an attachment relationship, over time and in the context of sensitive caregiving the infant learns to trust, to wait for her needs to be satisfied. She can then manage anxiety and tolerate brief separation from the attachment figure or figures.

There are important developmental consequences of this sensitive and synchronised caregiver-infant interaction. When the caregiver is trusted by the infant to be available, the *attachment behavioural system* is not taking up energy and the *exploratory behavioural system* becomes the focus of activity. The infant is free to explore, be interested in and learn from her environment. In this way, the securely attached infant is said to be able to use the attachment figure as a *secure base* (Ainsworth et al 1978, Bowlby 1969) who can be relied on and returned to in times of stress. That liberating experience of a secure base, a core concept in attachment theory, over time becomes internalised through a process of *mental representation* as the infant matures, so that the physical presence of the caregiver becomes less necessary as the child moves through the toddler years. At times of stress, however, the child will continue to need access to their secure base attachment figure.

Because of the significance of mental representations, the formation of a secure attachment relies also on the quality of the child's thinking. As Howe et al (1999:21) put it, ' "Felt security" can therefore be experienced by the use of the growing capacity to "mentalise" '. The child's emerging ability to think about his or her own mind and the minds of others, a form of *metacognition*, has come to be called the *reflective function* or *mind-mindedness*. It has been shown to be associated with secure attachment, being a key feature of sensitive caregiving (Fonagy 1996, 1999, 2001). The caregiver's ability to think, to reflect on their own and other's feelings and to help the child to do the same, enables the child to regulate their emotions and become a more effective operator in the social world (Howe et al 1999). Understanding that others have thoughts and feelings that differ from your own is a necessary part of negotiating relationships inside and outside of the family.

The process of *attachment formation* begins at birth, when the newborn infant is alert to the messages they receive about themselves and the world around them as reflected through the face of the caregiver. Within days the infant will prefer the voice of the mother and within a month will show a preference for her face. By three months, the baby is increasingly selective, already beginning to smile less readily for strangers and targeting their attachment behaviours more accurately. By around six – seven months, infants will show a very distinct preference for a particular caregiver. From this point on, the parent - child relationship is increasingly in synchrony. The infant actively behaves in ways that attract the attention and concern of the caregiver or caregivers to whom they are selectively attached and the caregivers tune in to the infant's communications and needs. The infant protests and shows distress or anxiety about being separated from that caregiver. Around that time or a little later, the baby is likely to show clear signs of anxiety about or fear of strangers. There follows a period in which securely attached infants and toddlers build on this early relationship as they become increasingly interested in toys, play and peers, but their primary attachment relationships will remain key to their healthy development.

By the age of three and a half or so the child will reach the stage described as a 'goal corrected partnership' (Bowlby 1969). By this stage children who have been exposed to sensitive caregiving and have had their minds and behaviour thought about and understood become more sophisticated in understanding their caregiver's mind and behaviour. This is in turn reflected in their ability to adapt their own behaviour accordingly. The child understands, for example, that the caregiver has their own needs and moods and that demands are more likely to be received positively at one time than another. There is thus an increased likelihood of negotiation and co-operation between caregiver and child, a model of mutuality in relationships that will assist the child in making constructive relationships with their peers and with adults outside the family.

**Adaptation and the internal working model**

Key to this process of attachment formation, according to Bowlby (1969), is that the infant learns to organise their behaviour around the response that they get, to *adapt* to the

relationship environment in which they find themselves. Sensory messages are assessed, regulated, interpreted and then appraised. Felt appraisals give a value, such as 'nice mum' or 'bad baby'. Certain behaviours are then selected on the basis of these appraisals. This process is centred on the relationship with the primary caregiver, with the evaluation of self and others arising out of the quality of the caregiving behaviour. This process leads to the development of a cognitive structure, a set of mental representations of self, others and relationships, known as an *internal working model*, which becomes the framework for future appraisals and future behavioural responses.

> *Central to Bowlby's theory of the working model of the self and of the attachment figure is the idea that, over time, there is an inextricable intertwining of the working model of the self and of the attachment figure. Thus, a child whose attachment needs are rebuffed not only comes to develop a model of the mother as rejecting, but of himself as unworthy of love and attention. Conversely, a child whose needs for contact and comfort are consistently met comes to represent the mother as available and caring and himself as loveable.* (Belsky and Cassidy 1994: 376)

As George (1996: 412) puts it, 'The behavioural system is guided at the representational level'.

The internal working model is not fixed in early childhood, but can adapt and change. It is a 'working' model, as George (1996) and others emphasise.

> *The concept of the internal working model refers to the mental representation of past events and interpersonal interactions, the confirmation and / or revision of these mental representations in the light of current interpersonal experiences, in the service of preparedness for future diverse interpersonal experiences...The optimal function of these representations is to encode interactions in such a way that will facilitate an ability to accurately predict how important others will behave and how the self might feel, think and behave in response. This view assumes an ongoing interplay among emotion, cognition and behaviour in personality development.* (Steele and Steele 1994: 95)

However, although the internal working model can adapt and change, there is likely to be a degree of continuity arising from the fact that expectations of others are likely to prove self-fulfilling.

> It is a presumption of contemporary attachment theory that working models become so deeply ingrained that they influence feelings, thought and behaviour unconsciously and automatically. They do this, according to Bowlby, by directing the child's attention to particular actions and events in his world, by shaping what the child remembers and does not and, thereby, by guiding his behaviour towards others and, thus, theirs towards him.
> (Belsky and Cassidy 1994: 379)

This understanding of the likely persistence of relationship patterns is an important part of our understanding of what, for example, children bring into foster care from their diversely troubled backgrounds (Schofield et al 2000, Sinclair et al 2000) and has led to some specific attempts to analyse the consequences (Stovall and Dozier 1998). Children who are wary, suspicious and feel unlovable often behave in ways that provoke and perpetuate the rejection they most fear.

The emphasis on the internal working model as a *cognitive structure* interacting with emotion and behaviour requires a radical shift for social workers away from an exclusive emphasis on *feelings*, on children's happiness, anger or sadness. An emphasis on emotions has tended to dominate social work assessment, although connections between *thinking* and *feeling* have a long history in psychodynamic casework (Winnicott 1964). In attachment theory, the links between thoughts and feelings are central to Bowlby's original model and have remained at the heart of its development, since mental representations, as well as feelings, drive the internal working model and have direct consequences in behaviour.

From a wide literature, George (1996: 413) summarises the agreed characteristics of internal working models in a way that demonstrates the concept and its developmental implications.

*First, they are derived from experiences with the attachment figure. Second, they consist of mental structures, rules or postulates that are abstracted into a collective perceptual record of interactive experience and affect... Third, internal working models involve defensive processes that influence how the individual perceives and remembers his or her experiences (Bowlby 1973, Main, Kaplan and Cassidy 1985). Fourth, although internal working models become increasingly stable, they can be changed to accommodate new experiences. In childhood, representational models may be changed as a function of experience with the parent; in adulthood, mental representations may be changed at the cognitive level, that is by thinking about the relationship itself.*

Note here the role of memory in laying down mental representations. This will be an important part of making sense of how adults think about attachment relationships and why adults tell the stories they tell about significant relationships in childhood. Important here also is the idea that working models change to accommodate new experiences, which suggests a window of opportunity for shifts towards security in the context of subsequent relationships, whether in the birth family or in substitute family or residential care. However, the existence of the defensive processes that are associated with insecure attachment patterns suggests why such shifts often prove so difficult to achieve.

# II

## SECURE AND INSECURE PATTERNS OF ATTACHMENT: MEASUREMENT AND DEVELOPMENTAL ROUTES

Having described some of the core concepts in attachment theory, it is necessary to understand how certain patterns that arise from different experiences of caregiving have been identified and classified and then to outline the developmental route through each secure and insecure pattern. It is important to understand the cognitive, emotional and behavioural characteristics of each developmental stage in each pattern. Extra attention will be paid to disorganised patterns, since so many children who cause concern to social workers and other professionals have experienced abuse or neglect (Schofield et al 2000) and so many maltreated children, in excess of 80% (Howe et al 1999), are likely to be classified as disorganised.

From the outset, attachment theory was developed by Bowlby in order to explain psychopathology as well as health (Bowlby 1944, 1951). The use of attachment theory to understanding individual differences was greatly enhanced by the work of Mary Ainsworth, whose observational studies with mothers and infants in Uganda were followed by the development of the 'Strange Situation' in the United States (Ainsworth et al 1978). The Strange Situation is an experimental procedure which measures in infancy the different secure and insecure patterns of attachment that develop in the context of different kinds of caregiving. This method for assessing attachment security in infants was developed around infants' reactions to caregivers, to separation from caregivers, to strangers and to reunion with caregivers following brief separations. Infants are taken through a series of brief events of separation and reunion which should 'activate the infant's attachment behavioural system' (George 1996: 414). Their behaviour is video recorded and analysed, to examine what has been revealed about the infant's mental representations. As Steele and Steele (1994: 95) have described it, the Strange Situation is a 'window on the child's internal working model of the child-caregiver relationship'. Each behaviour pattern in the child can be understood in relation to the quality of caregiving and its consequence for the child's behavioural strategies, as then reflected in the Strange Situation. Through the Strange Situation research, Ainsworth (1978) identified three patterns; secure (B), insecure -

avoidant (Λ) and insecure - ambivalent/resistant (C). Subsequent study of the children unclassified initially led to the identification of an insecure disorganised/disoriented (D) pattern (Main and Solomon 1986). (These patterns are described below).

As children move from infancy to pre-school and early middle childhood, it becomes necessary for researchers to use other methods of gaining access to the child's internal working model and attachment patterns (George 1996). This is most commonly achieved through projective tests. The use of narrative story stems (Solomon and George 1991, Solomon et al 1995) in particular has proved a particularly rich source of material and has given access to children's mental representations so that children, usually aged between 4 and 8, can be classified into secure and insecure patterns. In this procedure, children are presented with a doll family and the beginning of a story. The children are then invited to show and tell the researcher what they think will happen next.

As in the Strange Situation, the content of the story stems are designed to create some kind of attachment related anxiety. This will prompt the child to complete the story in ways which reveal their mental representation of the relationships between self and caregivers. For example, one story has a child spilling a drink while the family are watching television and another has a child falling down in the park and hurting his knee. In the analysis of the child's stories, there is particular interest in 'the degree to which the child represents adults as comforting and capable of caregiving as compared to injuring or neglectful' (Steele et al 1999: 20). There is also interest in the extent to which dramas and crises in the narrative are resolved. There have been a number of accounts of the use of the story stems and variations in the content of stories, generally drawing on the MacArthur Story Stem Battery of childhood narratives, but also developing other stories appropriate to the group of children (Bretherton et al 1990, Buchsbaum et al 1992, Oppenheim et al 1997, Steele et al 1999). This procedure has not widely been used by social work researchers, although Schofield et al (2000) used story stems in their research with foster children as a way of eliciting attachment-related material. They discovered that many foster children found it difficult to express ideas and feelings about parent figures directly in conversation with the researcher,

so the hypothetical and projective nature of the story stems often proved far more revealing about their mental representations of caregiver-child relationships.

Categorising attachment patterns in older middle childhood/early adolescence has proved more problematic, since children may be less comfortable with doll figures but are often not able to use adult schedules. A number of research interviews for children are now being developed which draw to a varying extent on the Adult Attachment Interview framework (see below) (Target et al in preparation, Steele and Steele personal communication). These require children aged 8-14 to be able to articulate an account of themselves, their friendships and their caregiving experiences in ways which allow researchers to classify their attachment patterns. The interviews are coded in relation to specific features such as coherence, self-esteem, the availability of a secure base and so on.

The instrument most commonly used in research for classifying the attachment patterns of adults is the Adult Attachment Interview (AAI) (George et al 1985, Main and Goldwyn 1984-1994). It is a semi-structured interview which although asking apparently simple questions about childhood and significant relationships, has the effect of 'surprising the unconscious'. The AAI also raises anxiety levels to a certain degree and 'provokes a discourse of attachment related memories' which reveals how the adult is organising thoughts and feelings and using 'different strategies or rules to access, process and express attachment related material' (Main 1995: 420). Adults are asked, for instance, to respond to the question, 'Can you give me five adjectives to describe your relationship with your mother in childhood?' They are then asked to give examples for each word. There are also specific questions about separations, losses and abuse in childhood. Coding of the interview transcript relies less on the content of the story than on the manner of its telling, in particular its coherence. It is through the analysis of the fine detail of the language used and the pattern of response and conversational interaction with the interviewer that it is possible to classify according to the different secure and insecure patterns. This is not a tool for use by social work practitioners in their everyday work. It is very time consuming to administer, transcribe and rate and to qualify to undertake the AAI rating requires a lengthy

training process. However, it is important to understand the principles of the AAI since it has been the basis of so much attachment research.

The evidence of the correlation between the adult attachment pattern of caregivers and the attachment pattern of their infants has been very influential in our understanding of intergenerational links. Fonagy et al (1991a) found that maternal representations of attachment as reflected in the Adult Attachment Interview predicted subsequent infant secure and insecure attachment patterns at 12 months in 75% of cases. As Hesse (1999) puts it, what is most striking about this association is that the *discourse* in which an adult presents his or her life narrative (regardless of the life content) predicts the *behaviour* of the infant in the Strange Situation at one year in highly specific ways. The combination of internal coherence, consistency and collaboration in a speaker's discourse regarding attachment predicts that speaker's likely capacity to impart security to an infant.

It is important to bear in mind that adults who have experienced loss, neglect or abuse in childhood will not necessarily be rated as insecure on the AAI. What matters is how those experiences have been processed, at the time and since. It is this which will be determining the current internal working model, the mental representations of self and relationships, and which will demonstrate how relationships are appraised and the behaviour/discourse that flows from that appraisal. For some adults there may be evidence that at the level of mental representations, the individual's current state of mind, it has been possible to reflect on and evaluate difficult or even traumatic experiences in a relatively non-defended way (Main and Goldwyn scoring manual 1984-94). These adults may then be rated as free to evaluate/ secure autonomous because they demonstrate what is described as 'earned' security.

## Patterns of attachment – developmental routes

### *Secure and autonomous / free to evaluate*
Securely attached children (referred to as a B classification in childhood), who have experienced sensitive care, mentally represent others as loving and available and themselves as loved and effective. Secure children are able to manage their anxiety and trust the

availability of the caregiver. There are a number of dimensions of parenting that are likely to lead to this secure base experience. Ainsworth (1971) set out four dimensions:

- Sensitivity-insensitivity
- Acceptance-rejection
- Co-operation-interference
- Accessibility-ignoring.

For secure attachments to develop in infancy, caregivers need to be sensitive to the child's signals, be able to see the world from the child's point of view and to have the ability to respond appropriately; to accept the child, both the good and the bad aspects, and the child's dependency; to promote co-operation and autonomy rather than conflict; and to be accessible to the child's signals of distress or sociability (see Howe et al 1999, Schofield et al 2000 for further discussion of these dimensions). Because the caregiver is sensitive to their needs, reads their signals and provides a secure base, there is a predictability and a cognitive scaffolding for the child within which the child can learn to think about and make sense of other people's emotions, thoughts and behaviours. The child learns to reflect on the internal worlds of self and others (Fonagy 1996).

Secure infants in the Strange Situation play and explore confidently in the presence of their caregiver. They show varying degrees of distress at separation but at reunion they demonstrate their trust in their caregiver as a secure base by settling quickly and returning to play. It is this reunion behaviour that is particularly indicative of a secure attachment.

Older secure children in the primary school years use their social skills to develop constructive relationships with peers as well as adults (Grossman and Grossman 1991). Because they are not preoccupied with attachment anxieties about the availability of the attachment figure, they are also free to learn and benefit from schooling. In addition their capacity to think logically and clearly will have been enhanced by their early caregiving experiences (Fonagy 1999).

Moving into adolescence, securely attached young people can rely further on their raised self-esteem and capacity to think in the context of a secure internal working model. Facing the major stress of separation and independence, their emotional and cognitive resources are tested in a way which early relationships enable them to handle. Adolescence is a time for establishing a sense of self in relation to the outside world (Erikson 1969). As at any stage of transition, there is the potential for increased anxiety. Negotiation of relationships in terms of dependence and independence, separateness and connectedness, will draw on those secure internal working models as teenagers try to make sense of who they are and where they are going in their lives. As Howe (1995: 133) suggests:

> The more secure the child's attachment history, the easier it is for him or her to separate and achieve an independent, well-integrated personality. If security leads to coherent personality structures and if they in turn promote social competence and confidence, adolescents with secure attachments have a deeply founded and well-integrated personality which is able to handle the demands of separation and independence and relationships beyond the family.

With these kinds of characteristics, particularly the capacity to think through situations and to be flexible, the secure adolescent moving into adulthood will be categorised as 'Free to evaluate' (F is the adult classification) or sometimes 'Secure-autonomous'. They are more likely to be able to form and sustain mutually rewarding relationships. Such adults can access their childhood memories, positive and negative and are able to evaluate them non-defensively. In the Adult Attachment Interview secure adults show these qualities in the way in which they reflect on their childhood and current relationships. They are able to recollect their parents as having both strengths and weaknesses, for example, and give examples of both. Their accounts are relevant, succinct and coherent.

As parents, secure autonomous adults are able to offer the sensitivity which they are most likely to have experienced in childhood or may have experienced since. George (1996) has called this group of mothers 'secure base'. Their capacity to build mutually rewarding relationships, to reflect on their own and others thoughts and feelings, is now a feature of their caregiving behaviour.

### *Avoidant, defended and dismissing*

Those infants whose caregivers reject or ignore them when they make demands, learn that the best way to achieve at least some proximity to the caregiver is to shut down on feelings, to minimise expressions of distress, to be self-reliant. Deactivating the attachment system is safer. The infant with an avoidant (A) pattern, therefore, effectively reduces the likelihood of hostility and maintains some kind of proximity, but denies and defends against feelings of need and hurt. The infant may seek comfort and satisfaction from objects rather than people, but play is not as rich, creative and imaginative as the play of a secure child who is not working so hard to screen out emotion (Greenberg et al 1991). In the Strange Situation the avoidant infant appears relatively indifferent to the mother's presence or absence, although physiologically they are highly aroused.

As the child grows through the pre-school years and into middle-childhood, the tendency to retreat into mental activity and to be self-reliant may prove constructive to some extent in school settings, although relationships will continue to be cool and distant. The child may be *compulsively compliant,* will inhibit anger in particular, when in the presence of more powerful or perhaps frightening adults, but may be aggressive when dominant, such as when with peers at school or younger children in the foster home. Although this pattern is called *avoidant,* it is important to bear in mind that the behaviour is not intended to 'avoid' relationships, it is simply the best and safest strategy to get whatever relationship can be achieved with rejecting or unresponsive carers. The child may be highly aroused and anxious about the threat of separation, but has learned not to show feelings. Unfortunately, the repression of the full range of feelings leaves them often unable to manage their own feelings flexibly or to read the feelings of others. Just as their parents became irritated by their expressions of emotion, so they in turn start to become irritated by expressions of feelings and needs in others, adults and their peers. This can then lead to outbursts of anger.

In adolescence, as stressed above, the question of impending separation is likely to raise anxiety.

*Adolescents who have experienced insecure and anxious attachment histories find both separation and the requirement to meet their relationship needs outside the family more difficult and disturbing.* (Howe et al 1999: 133)

The expectations of intimacy in relationships presents the avoidant adolescent with a dilemma. The impulse is to defend against the anxiety by minimising the importance of attachments and being self-reliant and emotionally distant. Crittenden (1995) argues that avoidant children may have particular problems in adolescence, because such defended children find it hard to tolerate the intimacy expected when partner relationships develop. She suggests that they may become isolated or promiscuous, achieving physical intimacy but remaining emotionally distant. They may throw themselves into academic work or lose themselves in depression or drug and alcohol abuse.

In adulthood, their responses in the Adult Attachment Interview reflect this dismissing (Ds), defended strategy in the manner in which childhood memories are recalled and described (Main and Goldwyn 1984-94). Parents may be idealised, but accounts of parents as loving are unconvincing and incoherent. Evidence in the form of stories to support their claims is lacking and significant losses are minimised. The more serious the parental rejection, the more energy and effort needs to go into defensively excluding that memory and persuading the interviewer of the truth of the idealised picture. This pattern can be very difficult for social workers to spot, whether in assessing birth parents or prospective foster or adoptive parents. Often the worker may feel unconvinced, but the account given of childhood is so positive that it is hard to see where the problem lies. This is not surprising, given that even when reading the AAI transcripts of dismissing adults systematically it can take a while to see that there are such gaps in the detail and such problems with coherence.

As parents, it would be expected that dismissing adults would minimise the emotional needs of the infant and find their emotional demands hard to accept or respond to. The tendency is to ignore the child or push them into independence, focusing perhaps on learning and mental development, to limit the emotional role that the caregiver is likely to have to play (Main 1995). The inevitable demands from the infant will provoke an angry outburst or

ignoring behaviour, either of which will confirm to the child that it is not safe to express needs.

In a caregiving interview, dismissing mothers of avoidant children deactivate the caregiving system. This group was called by George, 'rejecting'.

> *Most striking in the interviews of rejecting mothers was the exclusion of positive evaluations of themselves and their children. They emphasised the negative, portraying themselves and their children as unwilling and unworthy to participate in the relationship. Mothers described themselves as undesirable caregivers (for example, as strict, demanding, tough or impatient) and as uncomfortable with the maternal role. Similarly children were portrayed as undesirable (for example as a pain, monster or chore) and unwilling to respond to their mother's care. We believe that these negative evaluations both resulted from and permitted these mothers to dismiss their children's attachment needs and remain relatively uninvolved in the caregiving process. In terms of protection, the ultimate function of the caregiving system, the protection they provided was limited. For example, one rejecting mother was afraid that her child would have a swimming accident. Instead of supervising the child while she swam, however, the mother described how she napped indoors, reporting that she was confident that she would hear if her child was in trouble (George 1996: 418)*

Such experiences are as confusing for children as they are for social workers. Is this mother concerned for her child or not? It is important to note here that difficulty in interpreting caregiving behaviours is not confined to those of birth parents. For example, assessments of foster carers who remain 'uninvolved' may be inclined to conclude that the carer is just playing a professional role rather than that this is a dismissing pattern in the carer.

### Insecure-ambivalent / resistant

Infants with an *ambivalent/resistant* (C) pattern have caregivers who are inconsistently responsive, unpredictable and insensitive (George 1996, Howe et al 1999). These infants therefore need to devote a great deal of energy to communicating their feelings and needs, and ensuring that they have their caregivers' attention. This behaviour becomes more persistent as a result of the experience of intermittent reinforcement. They become preoccupied with the availability of the caregiver, but become dissatisfied and distrusting of that availability. In the Strange Situation, these infants are more alert and anxious about the

availability of the caregiver and at the reunion after separation resist attempts of the caregiver to reassure them and do not settle easily.

These infants maximise expressions of distress, but in time as they become of pre-school age their appeals to the caregiver for attention become associated with anger, as they realise that they are not their caregiver's priority. This pattern is therefore called ambivalent/resistant or coercive to reflect the way in which displays of need and displays of anger alternate as they try to force caregivers into giving them care and attention, even if that attention is negative. This hyperactivation of the attachment system leads to the deactivation of the exploratory system. The domination of affect, in the context of preoccupation with the caregiver's availability, thus reduces the child's capacity to learn.

As the child moves into the school years, he or she continues to be preoccupied, agitated and, at times, distressed and clingy, but the strategies may become rather more organised and sophisticated. The child learns to use charming or coy behaviour (Crittenden 1995), simultaneously appealing to and placating caregivers, alternating with coercive behaviours when disappointed or rejected. The child often switches between the two, as a way of breaking through the caregiver's lack of interest and involvement while protecting themselves from the caregiver's irritation. These coy/coercive strategies may work at times, but inevitably the caregiver becomes angry at the child's insistent, demanding and often manipulative behaviour, thus making the child more anxious, more demanding and more coercive. In some cases, this cycle may lead to aggression by the child or against the child. Where the caregiving is more severely *physically neglectful*, the child may simply sink into a depressed state (Crittenden 1995, Howe et al 1999). Some caregiver-child relationships are more explosive, others are more helpless and hopeless. In all cases, the child remains preoccupied with relationships and is likely to represent themselves as weak and unlovable with others as desired but unpredictable and lacking interest in them. The fact that caregivers are so unpredictable also means that the children distrust cognition. Mental processes are not to be trusted - only raised feelings are viewed as effective.

Crittenden (1995) would argue that it is in the school age years that coercive children have specific problems with adjustment as their preoccupation with and disappointment in relationships makes them troubled, angry and resentful. For these children (and their social workers) it is difficult to make sense of the parents' behaviour. Parents might at times be extremely effusive and sentimental about the child and yet not follow through in terms of concerned or sensitive caregiving behaviour. This gets played out quite often around contact for looked after children, who often remain painfully optimistic in spite of the evidence that their parent is not be able to sustain their commitment (Schofield et al 2000).

In school, preoccupation with attachment related issues means that these children have poor concentration. The anxiety about caregiver availability, the lack of a secure base and the distrust of thinking in favour of feeling, together leads to a lack of interest in and application to school work. Coy / coercive strategies learned in the relationship with the caregiver feature also with teachers and friends. Teachers experience them as needy but often irritating. Potential friends may be confused and overwhelmed by the coy-coercive behaviours. Other children may be attracted at first to a child who appears to be the life and soul of the party and who is offering to be their best friend. But they are then made uncomfortable by the child 'blowing hot and cold' and they can find themselves switching from being treated as best friend to becoming worst enemy.

In adolescence, anxious reactions to impending separation are likely to lead to an intensification of the familiar strategy - emotions are raised, coercive behaviours towards the caregiver persist and life can be very turbulent. Problems with peers become problems with partners as they move into adult life. These relationships will be dominated by the need to find the perfect partner and the distress of feeling that everyone lets them down. In the Adult Attachment Interview, adults are said to show a preoccupied anger, with entangled, enmeshed (E) patterns in relationships. As Hesse (1999: 398) puts it, preoccupied speakers are often 'unable to maintain a focus or to contain his or her responses to a given question'. In their accounts of childhood they show their preoccupation with relationships and also the strong sense of love-hate, the splitting of good and bad. Language may be sentimental or cliché-ridden but then slip into anger and resentment for all the remembered slights. There

may be excessive talk of family feuds and so on. As with ambivalent younger children in the story stems, positive and negative feelings are not integrated, with no acknowledgement made that other people, and themselves, can have some good and some bad qualities simultaneously. The quality of the account is confused, ambiguous and overlong.

As parents themselves, the legacy of all that need, anger and disappointment can lead to high expectations initially of what the baby will bring into their lives. But this cannot be matched by any consistent commitment of emotion or energy and interest. The child makes demands and inevitably disappoints too. Without intervention with caregiver and child, the cycle is likely to continue. In the caregiving interview, George (1996: 412) offers the following analysis of these entangled, preoccupied parents.

> *The defensive style of ambivalent mothers was cognitive disconnection. We called this group of mother 'uncertain'. In response to questions asking them to describe caregiving situations, they defensively disconnected and separated negative evaluations from the child and from memories of providing care. These mothers described their children in positive, even glowing terms; for example, children were seen as perfect, well-mannered, honest, fair, sensitive and altruistic. Caring for the child was portrayed as fun and the relationship filled with happiness. On some occasions during the interview, however, negative evaluations of the child emerged suddenly. The mother would describe the child as difficult, immature, angry, petulant or moody and she would appear to be confused and uncertain about the cause of the child's behaviour. This was often due to their failure to recognise events or dangers. In other instances, uncertain about how to provide effective care, mothers remained watchful and delayed taking action until forced to do so.*

This confused and inconsistent presentation makes it difficult for social workers to assess the parenting or make sense of the contradictory accounts of the child.

It is important to bear in mind that these parents will also be looking to social workers to recognise their needs and meet them. Such parents may greet a new social worker as special and the best one they've had - but when demands fail to be met, as they inevitably will be since what is wanted is unconditional love, the social worker too will find themselves on the receiving end of angry and at times coercive behaviour.

## Disorganised/unresolved patterns

Both avoidant and ambivalent patterns identified by Ainsworth are organised responses or defensive strategies. As George (1996: 414) put it,

> *Despite their anxiety, avoidant and ambivalent infants have been able to adapt to their parents and select, evaluate and modify their behaviour in a manner that allows them to achieve proximity and contact when needed.*

But there were a group of children who did not fit the A (avoidant), B (secure) or C (ambivalent/resistant) patterns in the Strange Situation, because they lacked a behavioural strategy to manage the situation (Main and Solomon 1986).

> *The infant displays disorganised and/or disoriented behaviours in the parent's presence during the Strange Situation suggesting a lapse of behavioural strategy. For example, the infant may freeze with a trance-like expression, hands in air, or may move away from the parent to the wall, turning the head away while crying.* (Main 1994).

Infants with a disorganised (D) pattern are likely to have parents or caregivers who are unpredictable, insensitive *and* rejecting. Fear seems to play a major part in the genesis of this pattern: fear in the child, fear of the caregiver, fear in the caregiver (Main and Hesse 1990). Caregivers may be frightening or frightened, violent themselves or victims of violence or traumatic loss, in the past or the present. They are experiencing unresolved trauma or loss. Such caregivers become a source of fear and anxiety in the child's environment rather than offering protection from anxiety. Infants have no strategy for dealing with or protecting themselves in this situation. They cannot read and make sense of this frightening and unpredictable environment and have few behavioural options available to them. Therefore their behaviour is truly disorganised, chaotic and random - emotions are unregulated, they may cry ceaselessly. This is why young infants are so much at risk from parents who themselves cannot regulate affect, anxiety and anger in particular, and are struggling to parent babies who become anxious, chaotic and unrewarding.

Not all disorganised children have been maltreated but since in excess of 80% of maltreated children may be disorganised (Howe et al 1999), it is particularly relevant for social workers

to understand this pattern in some detail. As maltreated, disorganised children move through the toddler years, they show signs of paradoxical approach / avoidance behaviours.- tempted to seek seek comfort but moving away to avoid hurt. Over time they have to develop a range of survival strategies, built not so much around achieving proximity - since proximity is uncomfortable and may be dangerous - but intended to enable the child to control their environment so that they can *be or at least feel safe* (Crittenden and Claussen 1999). This need to organise behaviour in the face of danger takes us back to the evolutionary heart of attachment theory and explains otherwise irrational behaviour. Some children for example develop obsessional behaviours, because the behaviour appears to have magical protective qualities. Crittenden (2000) gave the example of a child who twiddled her hair on one occasion when she thought her mother was about to strike her. Her mother did not strike her and the child twiddled her hair repeatedly on subsequent occasions, seeing this as a source of protection.

It is with this group of children that we are likely to see some of the most difficult behaviours to fathom, as children often show *compulsive compliance* in the presence of the abuser. They adopt false selves (Winnicott 1965), showing bright smiling faces and, as soon as they have speech, insist that all is well. This process is in evidence from as early as the second year of life and it is consistent with other developmental features, such as children's talk about their internal states.

> *The fact that maltreated children speak less about their negative internal states than do non-maltreated children is consistent with the findings of Crittenden and DiLalla (1988), who reported that during the latter half of the second year of life some maltreated children learn not only to inhibit negative affect but also to display positive affect.* (Toth et al 1997: 783)

For the school age child, the use of projective story stems has been particularly useful in gaining access to the disorganised child's mental representations, their 'incoherent and chaotic' internal working models (George 1996: 414).

*The doll play stories of disorganised 6-year-olds revealed internal working models of attachment in which parents and adults failed to provide protection and safety. Their stories depicted parents and other adult figures as frightened, frightening, chaotic and / or helpless. Dangerous events (for example, the family car raging out of control, or an abusive baby-sitter or parent) were left unresolved. Adults who potentially might have been of help were depicted as helpless to get assistance from others, to control their behaviour or the events around them. Some children, for example, were thrown in jail or beaten. In some instances, the child's only recourse was to keep secrets or hide. Stories often ended in chaos and disintegration of the self or the family....Flooded by pain, anger, fear and distress, their representational models become dysregulated; they are left feeling helpless and out of control.* (George 1996: 416)

This has been quoted at length because it is highlights the way in which the impact of different caregiving experiences, in this case those often typical of maltreatment, become built into the internal working model (see also Solomon et al 1995). These feelings of fear and helplessness then go on to affect expectations of new situations, such as the move into a foster family or to a new school. However, what is happening behaviourally may not obviously be reflecting the fear and chaos that the story stems reveal as existing in the internal world of the child. It is not surprising that in child death inquiries, children such as Kimberley Carlile (London Borough of Greenwich 1987), Sukina (Stone 1991) and the older siblings of Paul (Bridge Child Care Consultancy 1995), living in the most extreme situations of abuse or neglect, were found to have smiled and that this reassured professionals that all was well.

Whether the caregiver is themselves frightened, perhaps a victim of domestic violence or someone who has unresolved trauma from their own childhood, or is frightening, one of the paradoxes explained by attachment theory is that there is likely to be a role reversal, the child may become a *compulsive caregiver*, suppressing their own needs and paying watchful attention to, caring for and/or placating the adult. The parent's sense of the child as powerful is matched with the child's representation of the relationship as a role reversal. This is, as George (1996: 419) puts it (citing Solomon and George 1994), 'a relationship imbalance that allows the child to care precociously for the self by caring for the mother'.

These disorganised children will often be showing distress in other ways. The associated dysfunctional behaviours form a long list (see Howe et al 1999: 136). They include superficial charm with strangers; poor impulse control and restlessness; dislike of being touched or held; high levels of rage/anger/violence; manipulative lying; stealing and conduct disorders; abnormal eating patterns; lack of conscience; cruelty towards animals; preoccupation with death and gore. In all this frightening confusion, one predominant strategy emerges - the child begins to believe that the only way of surviving is to be in control of the self and other people, whatever form that control may take. The child begins to represent the self as powerful and bad but also, defensively, as strong and invulnerable.

> *In summary, children classified as disorganised and controlling, aggressive and defended, punitive and fearful:*
> - *avoid closeness in relationships (intimacy implying fear and danger)*
> - *control rather than be controlled (because they fear remaining at the mercy of an unpredictable dangerous world)*
> - *defensively exclude and deny hostile, distressing and frightening experiences - this includes assuming a self that is seen as powerful, aggressive, invulnerable and punitive, able to attack and keep dangerous threatening forces at bay....* (Howe et al 1999: 148)

Trusting others who may try to offer good care, such as foster carers or adoptive parents, is too risky. Such children have mental representations which are so distinctively distorted that far from being able to accept appropriate care when it is offered by carers, they will misinterpret what is happening, reframing it to fit their own expected model.

> *The individual may so distrust both affect and cognition that even discrepant information may not trigger the mind to re-explore reality. Instead the mind may determine that this too is trickery and deception or that the risk of mistakenly responding as though it were true is too great to be tolerated. In such cases, the representation of reality is like a false, inverted mirror image in which good and bad, true and false are reversed.* (Crittenden 1995: 401)

This is close to what we know occurs when previously maltreated children are placed in new families (Fahlberg 1994, Howe and Fearnley 1999, Schofield 2000).

Through school years into adolescence, children with such behaviours and such a distorted approach to others are likely to have difficulties not only in relationship to birth or substitute parents but also to teachers and with peers. As Cicchetti and Toth (1995: 552) put it, 'It is not surprising that children who have been maltreated are at extremely high risk for failure at school'. In adolescence they are likely to struggle because they continue to lack trust and their fearfulness makes them uncomfortable with others and inclined to become controlling. The dysfunctional behaviours may also lead on to externalising problems with aggression and offending and/or internalising problems with drug misuse, depression and self-harm.

Those adults whose state of mind remains affected by the trauma of the loss of an attachment figure or abuse in childhood are classified as 'unresolved' (U) in the Adult Attachment Interview. They show 'lapses in the monitoring of reason or discourse' at certain points in the AAI (Main 1996). These lapses may be just a phrase or a few sentences or an exceptionally long pause during the interview, but it indicates that subjects remain confused and disorganised. Although classified as unresolved in the AAI, these adults will also be assigned to a best fitting alternative classification - so, U/Ds, U/E or even U/F, where an otherwise secure, 'free to evaluate' adult may score highly overall on coherence, yet still have lapses triggered by discussion of traumatic events.

As parents, research suggests, unresolved adults have significant problems. George calls this group of unresolved mothers 'helpless', because of the caregiving that flows from their representational models.

> *Feeling helpless and out of control, they described themselves as lacking effective and appropriate resources to handle the child, often describing harsh punishment, hysteria, and depression. Their children were also evaluated as being out of the control of their care. Some children were portrayed as wild, chaotic and beyond help...*(George 1996: 419)

Parental feelings of helplessness can be associated with fear of the child, but also with anger and aggression towards the child which may be acted out or may lead to total rejection of the child.

These different secure and insecure attachment patterns are distinguished by the extent to which they enable the child to cope with anxiety, force the child to construct an organised defence or leave children with behaviours that control others and avoid intimacy. As Howe (1995: 89) puts it in summary,

> *It has to be emphasised that children's behaviour in relationships which are defined as maladaptive is only viewed as such as far as future social competence is concerned. The behaviour of insecurely attached children is an adaptive response within the context of the relationship in which they find themselves. The behaviour adopted is a defensive strategy developed by the child in order to cope with feelings of anxiety, uncertainty and fear.*

# CONCLUSION

## USING ATTACHMENT THEORY IN PRACTICE

Attachment theory has relevance for all aspects of child care social work practice: family support; work with children with disabilities; child protection; court work; family placement; leaving care; youth offending. It also has relevance for all stages in the social work process from referral, through assessment, intervention and review (see Howe et al 1999 for a practice and assessment model that is based on attachment theory). This universality is not surprising given the universality of the need to promote healthy development and rewarding social relationships among vulnerable children and young people. However, as the complexity of the theoretical framework outlined above would suggest, it is extremely important to ensure that the theory is well-understood when applying it to individual cases.

Detailed and accurate evidence regarding the case and a degree of caution about labelling are also advisable because, as attachment theory itself suggests, the more serious the case the more confusing the picture may be. Caregivers who are particularly harmful or frightening to children often give very confusing messages and have strategies that may control, manipulate and intimidate social workers and other professionals. Children who have been maltreated have also learned to mislead and confuse in order to remain in control. Thus we have the paradox that those situations where making the right decision is a matter of greatest significance are also the most difficult to disentangle, even with the benefit of attachment theory. It is thus all the more important to ensure that all of the complex behaviours in family relationships are observed and described in ways that allow other professionals, as well as other social workers, to see the pattern of the behaviour and the way in which it may be related to the child's or the parent's relationship history. Patterns of events and relationships across time and across generations will also be of great importance. The theory is most helpful in the context of a through assessment of the present and the past.

In addition, it is important to bear in mind that many social work assessments are made for a multi-disciplinary audience or a social work audience with varying levels of understanding of developmental attachment theory. In preparing assessments, therefore, on which decisions about intervention will be based ( such as in need / family support decisions, child protection case conferences, court, looked after children reviews and adoption panels), it is important to start by describing the child's and the parents' *behaviour* and use the theory to help make sense of it rather than jumping to attachment terminology such as 'avoidant' or 'dismissing'. A child who appears self-reliant and does not show emotions in situations which are deemed to be distressing might be regarded by others as unaffected or even as a resilient child. Offering an attachment theory based explanation of the meaning of that behaviour as perhaps being a learned strategy for coping with rejection is more helpful than saying simply 'this is an avoidant child'. Effective use of attachment theory in practice requires the social worker to employ not only a good understanding of the theory but some strategies for using it in ways that make sense to other professionals.

Attachment theory is primarily a theory for understanding and therefore seems particularly helpful in assessment. However, it does have implications for intervention. As Howe et al (1999:246) put it:

> *Broadly speaking, interventions seek to modify the quality of interaction between children and their social environment (which includes parents, family, peers and other adults).*

The message here for social workers is that although directly seeking to improve the quality of interaction between children and their caregivers is an obvious focus for intervention based on attachment theory, the child's sense of security, self-esteem and self-efficacy may also be increased by intervening in the systems around the family, for example providing social support to the mother (Crockenberg 1981), social work advocacy at school or funding a place for the child in an activity group.

In order to use attachment theory in practice it is essential that social workers not only master the detail and subtlety of the framework but also have ongoing support and supervision. Behaviours in troubled children and parents rarely point readily to a simple explanation. In addition, workers with distressed, anxious and angry families can easily be drawn into entangled family dynamics and find it harder to think about what is going on. Much time and thought has to go, therefore, into working out what is going on, both within the family and between the family and the worker. But if the theory is well understood and there is support available then, as Howe et al (1999:294) put it, it can free the worker to be both thoughtful and compassionate.

> *The ability to make intellectual sense of people in difficult and distressing and disturbed situations increases social workers' emotional availability. Theoretical understanding helps practitioners to stay with demanding cases and lessens the likelihood of a retreat into procedural ways of working.*

As child care social workers continue to define and defend their distinctive psychosocial professional identity in the multi-disciplinary networks around vulnerable children, a knowledgeable and sensitive use of developmental attachment theory has an important contribution to make.

# REFERENCES

Ainsworth, M. D. S., Bell, S. and Stayton, D. (1971) Individual differences in strange-situation behavior of one year olds. In Schaffer, H. (ed.) *The Origins of Human Social Relations,* New York: Academic Press, pp. 17-52.

Ainsworth, M. D. S., Blehar, M., Waters, E. and Wall, S. (1978) *Patterns of Attachment: A Psychological Study of the Strange Situation,* Hillsdale, NJ: Lawrence Erlbaum.

Belsky, J. and Cassidy, J. (1994) Attachment: Theory and Evidence, In Rutter, M. and Hay, D. (eds.) *Development through Life,* Oxford; Blackwell, pp. 373-402.

Bowlby, J. (1944) Forty-four juvenile thieves: their characters and home life. *International Journal of Psychoanalysis,* 25, pp. 1-57 and 200-228.

Bowlby, J. (1951) *Maternal Care and Mental Health,* Geneva: WHO.

Bowlby, J. (1969) *Attachment and Loss: Vol 1 Attachment,* London: Hogarth Press.

Bowlby, J. (1973) *Attachment and Loss: Vol II Separation, Anxiety and Anger,* London: Hogarth Press.

Bowlby, J. (1979) *The Making and Breaking of Affectional Bonds.* London: Tavistock.

Bowlby, J. (1980) *Attachment and Loss: Vol III Loss, Sadness and Depression,* London: Hogarth Press.

Bowlby, J. (1988) *A Secure Base: Clinical Applications of Attachment Theory,* London: Routledge.

Bretherton, I., Ridgeway, D. and Cassidy, J. (1990) Assessing internal working models of the attachment relationship: an attachment story completion task for three year olds. In Greenberg, M. T., Cicchetti, D. and Cummings, E. M. (eds.) *Attachment in the Preschool Years: Theory, research and intervention,* Chicago: University of Chicago Press, pp. 273-308.

Bridge Child Care Consultancy (1995) *Paul: Death through Neglect,* London: Published on behalf of Islington Area Child Protection Committee.

British Agencies for Adoption and Fostering (BAAF) (1999) *Preparation for Permanence: Assessment Preparation and Support - implications from research,* London: BAAF.

Bronfenbrenner, U. (1979) *The ecology of human development: Experiments by nature and design,* Cambridge, MA: Harvard University Press.

Buchsbaum, H. K., Toth, S. L., Clyman, R. B., Cicchetti, D. and Emde, R. N. (1992) The use of narrative story – stem technique with maltreated children: implications for theory and practice, *Development and Psychopathology,* 4, pp. 603-625.

Cairns K (2002) *Attachment, trauma and resilience* London: BAAF

Carlson, V., Cicchetti, D., Barnett, D. and Braunwald, K. G. (1989) Finding order in disorganisation: lessons from research on maltreated infants attachments to their caregivers. In Cicchetti, D. and Carlson, V. (eds.) *Child Maltreatment: Theory and research on the causes and consequences of child abuse and neglect.* Cambridge: Cambridge University Press, pp. 494-528.

Cicchetti, D. and Carlson, V. (eds.) (1989) *Child Maltreatment: Theory and research on the causes and consequences of child abuse and neglect.* Cambridge: Cambridge University Press.

Cicchetti, D. and Rogosch, F. A. (1997) The role of self-organisation in the promotion of resilience in maltreated children, *Development and Psychopathology,* pp. 797-815.

Cicchetti, D. and Toth, S. (1995) Child maltreatment and attachment organization: implications for intervention. In Goldberg, S., Muir, R. and Kerr, J. (eds.) *Attachment Theory: Social development and clinical perspectives,* Hillsdale, NJ: Analytic Press, pp. 279-308.

Crittenden, P. M. (1995) Attachment and psychopathology. In Goldberg, S., Muir, R. and Kerr, J. (eds.) *Attachment theory: Social, developmental and clinical perspectives,* Hillsdale, NJ: Analytical Press, pp. 367-406.

Crittenden, P. (2000) *Attachment and Maltreatment* Conference paper, BASPCAN London.

Crittenden, P. M. and DiLalla, D, (1988) Compulsive compliance: The development of an inhibitory coping strategy in infancy. *Journal of Abnormal Child Psychology,* 16, pp. 585-599.

Crittenden, P. M. and Ainsworth, M. D. S. (1989) Child maltreatment and attachment theory. In Cicchetti, D. and Carlson, V. (eds.) *Child Maltreatment: Theory and research on the causes and consequences of child abuse and child neglect,* Cambridge: Cambridge University Press, pp. 432-463.

Crittenden, P. M. and Claussen, A. H. (eds.) (1999) *The Organisation of attachment relationships: Maturation, Culture and Context,* Cambridge: Cambridge University Press.

Crockenberg, S. B. (1981) Infant irritability, mother responsiveness and social support influences on the security of infant-mother attachment, *Child Development,* 52, pp. 857-865.

Curtis Report (1946) *Report of the Care of Children Committee.*

Department of Health (1999) *The Government's Objectives for Children's Social Services,* London: Stationery Office.

Department of Health (2000) *Framework for the Assessment of Children in Need and their families* London: Stationery Office.

Fahlberg, V. ( 1994) *Child's Journey through Placement,* (2nd ed.) London: BAAF.

Fonagy, P. (1996) *Attachment and Theory of Mind: Overlapping Constructs?* Association of Child Psychology and Psychiatry Occasional Papers.

Fonagy, P. (1999) *Attachment, the development of the self and its pathology in personality disorders,* retrieved from the World Wide Web:
http:/www.psychomedia.it/pm/modther/probpsiter/fonagy-2.htm

Fonagy, P. (2001) *Attachment Theory and Psychoanalysis,* New York: Other Press.

Fonagy, P., Steele, H. and Steele, M. (1991a) Maternal representations of attachment during pregnancy predict the organisation of Infant-Mother attachment at one year of age. *Child Development,* 62, pp. 891-905.

Fonagy, P., Steele, H., Steele, M., Moran, G. S. and Higgett, A. (1991b) The capacity for understanding mental states: the reflective self in parent and child and its significance for security of attachment, *Infant Mental Health Journal,* 13, pp. 200-217.

George, C. (1996) A representational perspective of child abuse and prevention: Internal working models of attachment and caregiving. *Child Abuse and Neglect,* 20 (5), pp. 411-424.

George, C., Kaplan, N. and Main, M. (1985) *The Berkeley Adult Attachment Interview.* Unpublished Protocol Department of Psychology, University of California Berkeley.

George, C. and Solomon, J. (1989) Internal working models of caregiving and security of attachment at age 6, *Infant Mental Health,* 10, pp. 222-237.

George, C. and Solomon, J. (1996) Representational models of relationships: Links between caregiving and attachment. In George, C. and Solomon, J. (eds.) *Defining the caregiving system: Infant Mental Health,* 17, New York: Wiley, pp. 198-216.

Goldberg, S. (2000) *Attachment and Development,* London: Arnold.

Greenberg, M. T., Cicchetti, D. and Cummings, E. M. (eds.) (1990) *Attachment in the Preschool Years: Theory, Research and Intervention,* Chicago: University of Chicago Press.

Grossman, K. E. and Grossman, K. (1991) Attachment quality as an organiser of emotional and behavioural resources in a longitudinal population. In Parkes, C. M., Stevenson-Hinde, J. and Marris, P. (eds.) *Attachment across the life span.* Harmondsworth: Penguin, pp.93-114

Hesse, E. (1999) Discourse, Memory and the Adult Attachment Interview: A note with emphasis on the emerging cannot classify category, *Infant Mental Health Journal,* 17 (1) pp. 4-11.

Howe, D. (ed.) *Attachment and Loss in Child and Family Social Work.* Basingstoke: Avebury

Howe D (2001*)* Relating Theory to Practice in Davies M (2nd edition) *Blackwell Companion to Social Work* London, Blackwell Science

Howe, D. and Fearnley, S. (1999) Disorders of attachment and attachment therapy, *Adoption and Fostering,* 23 (2), pp. 19-30.

Howe, D., Brandon, M., Hinings, D. and Schofield, G. (1999) *Attachment Theory: Child Maltreatment and Family Support,* Basingstoke: Macmillan.

Main, M. (1991) Metacognitive knowledge, metacognitive monitoring and singular (coherent) vs. multiple (incoherent) model of attachment: findings and directions for future research. In Parkes, C. M., Stevenson-Hinde, J. and Marris, P. (eds.) *Attachment across the life-cycle,* London: Tavistock/Routledge, pp. 127-159.

Main, M. (1994) *A move to the level of representation in the study of attachment organisation: Implications for psychoanalysis,* Annual Research Lecture to the British Psycho-Analytical Society.

Main, M. (1995) Recent studies in attachment: overview with selected implications for clinical work. In Goldberg, S., Muir, R. and Kerr, J. (eds.) *Attachment Theory: Social, Developmental and Clinical Perspectives,* Hillsdale, NJ: The Analytic Press, pp. 407-474.

Main, M. and Goldwyn, R. (1984-94) *Adult Attachment Scoring and Classification System,* unpublished manuscript, Department of Psychology, University of California, Berkeley.

Main, M. and Hesse, E. (1990) Parents' unresolved traumatic experiences are related to infant disorganized attachment status: Is frightened and/or frightening parental behaviour the linking mechanism? In Greenberg, M., Cicchetti, D. and Cummings, E. M. (eds.) *Attachment in the Preschool Years: Theory, Research and Intervention,* Chicago: University of Chicago Press, pp. 161-182.

Main M, Kaplan N and Cassidy J (1985) Security in infancy, childhood and adulthood. In Bretherton I and Waters E (eds) *Growing Points of Attachment Theory and Research: Monographs of the Society for Research in Child Development* 50 (1-2. Serial No. 209)

Main, M. and Solomon, J. (1986) Discovery of an insecure-disorganised/disoriented attachment pattern. In Brazzelton, T. B. and Yogman, M. W. (eds.) *Affective Development in Infancy,* Norwood, NJ: Ablex, pp. 95-124.

Oppenheim, D., Emde, R. and Warren, S. (1997) Children's narrative representations of mothers: their development and associations with child and mother adaptation. In *Child Development*, 67, pp 541-556, Cited in Steele, M., Hodges, J., Kaniuk, J., Henderson, K., Hillman, S. and Bennett, P. (1999) The use of story stem narratives in assessing the inner world of the child: Implications for adoptive placements, In BAAF (1999) *Preparation for Permanence: Assessment Preparation and Support - implications from research*, London: BAAF.

Parker, R., Ward, H., Jackson, S., Aldgate, J. and Wedge, P. (1991) *Looking After Children: Outcomes in Child Care.* London: HMSO.

Schofield, G. (1998a) Inner and Outer Worlds : A psychosocial framework for child and family social work, *Child and Family Social Work,* 3 (1), pp. 57-68.

Schofield, G. (1998b) Making sense of the ascertainable wishes and feelings of insecurely attached children, *Child and Family Law Quarterly,* 10 (4), pp. 363-376.

Schofield G (2003) *Part of the Family: Pathways through Foster Care* London: BAAF

Schofield, G. and Brown, K. (1999) A family centre worker's role as a secure base for adolescent girls. *Child and Family Social Work,* 4 (1), pp. 21-31.

Schofield, G., Beek, M., Sargent, K. with Thoburn, J. (2000) *Growing up in Foster Care.* London: BAAF.

Solomon, J. and George, C. (1991) *Working models of attachment of children classified as controlling at age 6: Disorganization at the level of representation.* Paper presented at the biennial meeting of the Society for research in Child Development, April, Seattle WA. Cited in George, C. (1996) A representational perspective of child abuse and prevention: Internal working models of attachment and caregiving. *Child Abuse and Neglect,* 20 (5), pp. 411-424.

Solomon, J. and George, C. (1994) *Disorganization of maternal caregiving strategies: An attachment approach to role reversal* Paper presented at the meeting of the American Psychological Association, August. Los Angeles, CA. Cited in George, C. (1996) A representational perspective of child abuse and prevention: Internal working models of attachment and caregiving. *Child Abuse and Neglect,* 20 (5), pp. 411-424.

Solomon, J., George, C. and DeJong, A. (1995) Symbolic representation of attachment in children classified as controlling at age 6. Evidence of disorganization of representation strategies. *Development and Psychopathology,* 7, pp. 447-464.

Sroufe, I. A. (1997) Psychopathology as an outcome of development, *Development and Psychopathology,* 9 (2), pp. 251-266.

Steele, H. and Steele, M. (1994) Intergenerational Patterns of Attachment, *Advances in Personal Relationships,* 5, pp. 93-120.

Steele, M., Hodges, J., Kaniuk, J., Henderson, K., Hillman, S. and Bennett, P. (1999) The use of story stem narratives in assessing the inner world of the child: Implications for adoptive placements, in British Agencies for Adoption and Fostering *Preparation for Permanence: Assessment Preparation and Support - implications from research,* London: BAAF, pp. 19-27.

Stone, W. (1991) *Sukina: an evaluation report of the circumstances leading to her death,* London: Bridge Child Care Consultancy.

Stovall, K. C. and Dozier, M. (1998) Infants in Foster Care: An attachment perspective, *Adoption Quarterly,* 2 (1), pp. 55-87.

Target, M., Shmueli-Goetz, Y., Fonagy, P. and Datta, A. (in preparation) *Attachment representations in school age children: the development and validity of the Child Attachment Interview* (CAI), London: University College Unpublished manuscript. Cited in Fonagy, P. (2001) *Attachment Theory and Psychoanalysis,* New York: Other Press.

Toth, S., Cicchetti, D., Macfie, J. and Emde, R. (1997) Representations of self and other in the narratives of neglected, physically abused and sexually abuse preschoolers, *Development and Psychopathology,* 9 (4), pp. 781- 795.

Winnicott, C. (1964) *Child Care and Social Work,* Hitchin: Codicote Press.

Winnicott, D. (1965) *The Maturational Process and the Facilitative Environment.* New York: International Universities Press.

van IJzendoorn, M. H. and Bakermans-Kranenburg, M. J. (1996) Attachment representations in mothers, fathers, adolescents and clinical groups: a meta analytic search for normative data. *Journal of Consulting and Clinical Psychology,* 64, pp.8-21.